Senses

Lisa Greathouse

Consultant

Gina Montefusco, RN
Children's Hospital Los Angeles
Los Angeles, California

Publishing Credits

Dona Herweck Rice, *Editor-in-Chief*; Lee Aucoin, *Creative Director*; Don Tran, *Print Production Manager;* Timothy J. Bradley, *Illustration Manager*; Chris McIntyre, *Editorial Director*; James Anderson, *Associate Editor*; Jamey Acosta, *Associate Editor*; Jane Gould, *Editor*; Peter Balaskas, *Editorial Administrator*; Neri Garcia, *Senior Designer*; Stephanie Reid, *Photo Editor*; Rachelle Cracchiolo, M.S.Ed., *Publisher*

Image Credits

cover Ugurbariskan/iStockphoto; p.1 Ugurbariskan/iStockphoto; p.4 (top) Kokhanchikov/Shutterstock, (bottom) Torsten Schon/Shutterstock; p.5 (left) Torsten Schon/Shutterstock, (right) Avava/Shutterstock; p.6 Hydromet/Shutterstock; p.7 Blacqbook/Shutterstock; p.8 Stephanie Reid; p.9 (top) Stephanie Reid/Kapu/Shutterstock, (bottom) Alexander Hafemann/iStockphoto; p.10 (left) Margouillat Photo/Shutterstock, (right) svlumagraphica/Dreamstime; p.11 Gelpi/Shutterstock; p.12 Andreus/Dreamstime; p.13 DougSchneiderPhoto/iStockphoto; p.14 3445128471/Shutterstock; p.15 (top) Russell Athon/Dreamstime, (bottom) Tina Rencelj/Shutterstock; p.16 ImageDJ/Jupiter Image; p.17 Titov Andriy /Shutterstock; p.18 (left) Shelly Perry/iStockphoto, (right) Citi Jo/Shutterstock; p.19 (top) Redfrisbee/Shutterstock; (bottom left) Konovalikov Andrey/Shutterstock, (bottom middle) apdesign/Shutterstock, (bottom right) Marino/Shutterstock; p.20 Jean Schweitzer/iStockphoto; p.21 (top) Melanie DeFazio/Shutterstock, (bottom) Ivvv1975/Shutterstock; p.22 (left) Fuyu Liu/Shutterstock, (middle) Shariffc/Dreamstime, (right) Vasily Smirnov/Shutterstock; p.23 (top) Andrea Gingerich/iStockphoto, (left) Tatik22/Shutterstock, (center left) mrsnstudio/Shutterstock, (center right) Brocorwin/Shutterstock, (right) Serg64/Shutterstock; p.24 (left) Elena Stepanova/Shutterstock, (right) Kacso Sandor/Shutterstock; p.25 Dmitriyd/Shutterstock; p.26 (left) Maska82/Dreamstime, (right) Ugurbariskan/iStockphoto; p.27 (top) Bryngelzon/iStockphoto, (bottom) Kim Gunkel/iStockphoto; p.28 Rocket400 Studio/Shutterstock; p.29 Ana Clark; p.32 Drs. Jean Bennett and Al Maguire

Teacher Created Materials

5301 Oceanus Drive
Huntington Beach, CA 92649-1030
http://www.tcmpub.com
ISBN 978-1-4333-1429-2
© 2011 by Teacher Created Materials, Inc.
Reprinted 2012

Table of Contents

The Five Senses

People have five senses. We can see things. We can hear. We can smell things. We can taste. We can feel the things we touch.

taste

touch

hear

smell   see

What color is the sky? It is blue, of course! We know this because we see it with our eyes.

We learn a lot by using our eyes.

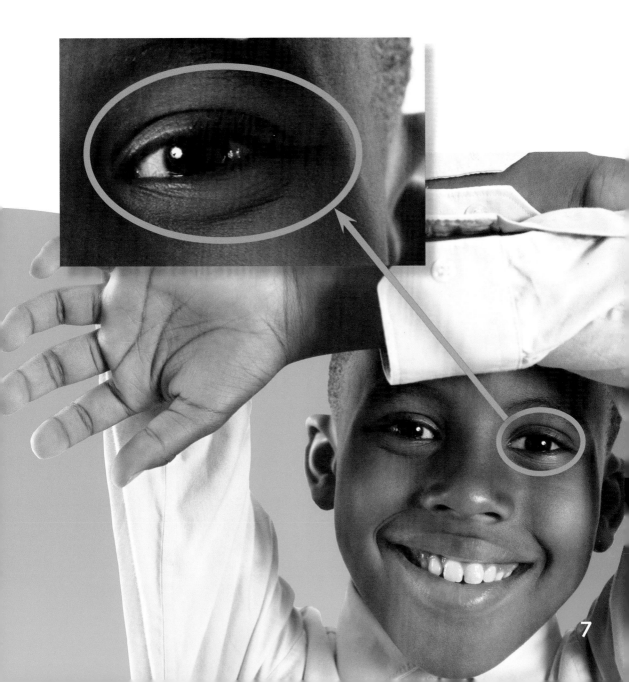

Eyes work like a camera. They take tiny pictures. But they take the pictures upside down!

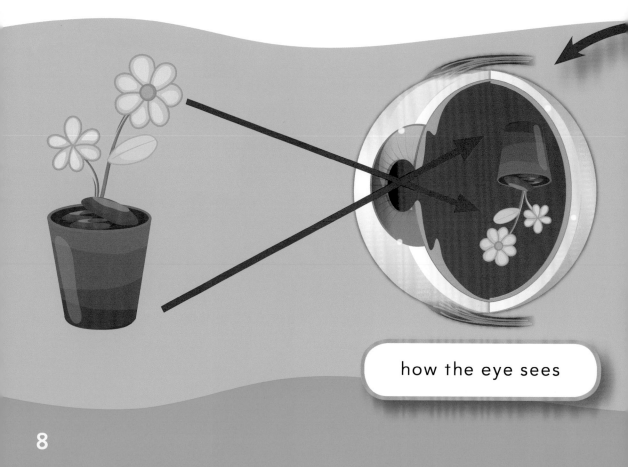

how the eye sees

Then a message is sent to the brain. Your brain tells you what you see, and flips the picture around!

It Is Okay to Cry
Tears wash your eyes—even when you blink.

What does a **siren** sound like? How about a dog barking?

Sounds travel through the air in **waves**. The sound waves go into your ears. They can warn you about danger.

Inside your ear, sounds hit your **eardrum**.

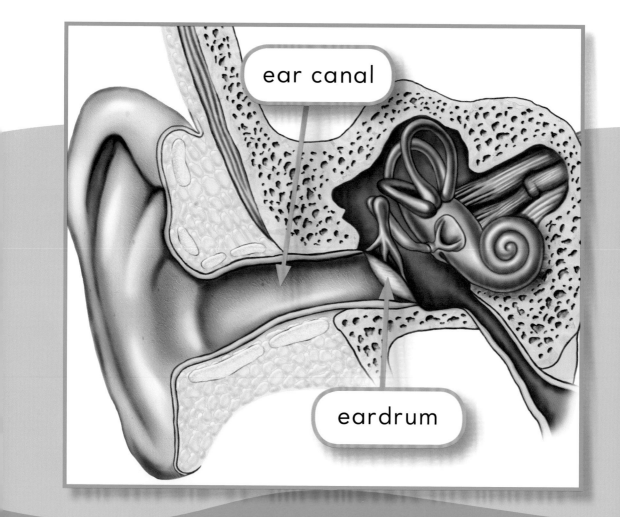

ear canal

eardrum

Nerves inside your ear send a message to your brain. Your brain tells you what you are hearing.

Fun Fact

The **wax** in your ears helps protect them and keep them clean.

Have you ever smelled a rotten egg?
That stinks!

How about cookies baking in the oven? Mmmm. They smell good!

How can you tell the difference? Your nose tells you!

Dogs use their noses all the time.

When you breathe, air goes into your nose through your nostrils.

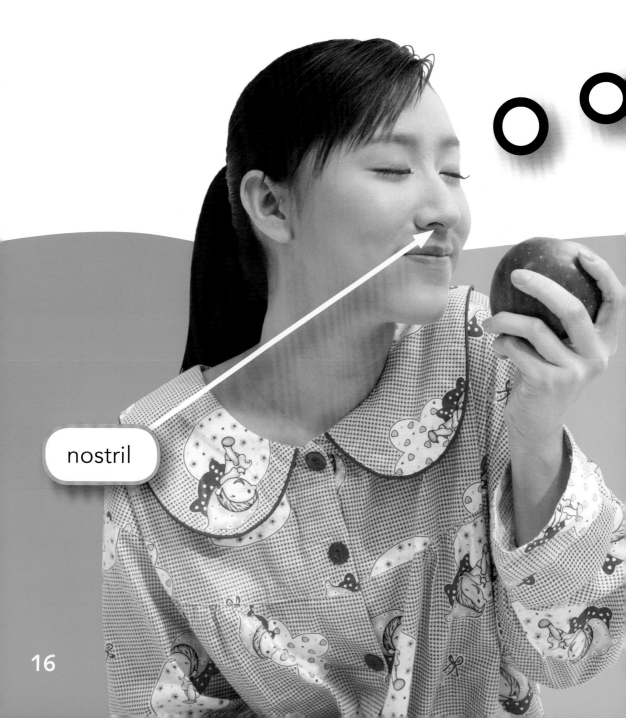

nostril

16

There are nerves inside your nose that send messages to your brain. Your brain tells you what you are smelling.

How does it feel when you pet a kitten?
How about when you touch a hot stove?

Your sense of touch tells you a lot about the world.

You touch with your skin. Nerves send messages to your brain.

Your brain tells you what you are touching. Is it soft or smooth? Hot or cold? Slimy or dry?

Fun Fact

Fingerprints are the tiny lines on the tips of your fingers. No two people have the same fingerprints!

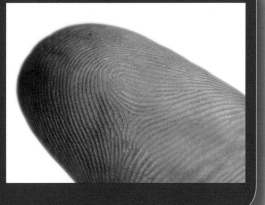

You taste with your tongue. Mmmm, that lollipop is yummy. Wow! That pepper is hot!

Life would be boring without the sense of taste!

There are tiny bumps all over your tongue. They are called **taste buds**.

bitter

not
many
taste
buds

sour

sour

salty/
sweet

This is what the taste buds on your tongue look like much larger.

Taste buds can sense four tastes. The tastes are sweet, sour, bitter, and salty. You taste them on different parts of your tongue.

Fun Fact
Catfish have taste buds all over their bodies!

Knowing Your World

What would life be like without your senses? What if you could not enjoy music? Or the taste of an apple?

Your senses help you know your world.
They help you enjoy it, too!

Science Lab: Brain Box

What is in the box? If you cannot see it, how can you know?

Materials:

- a box with a hole cut in the side for your hand
- six objects with different textures, such as a spoon, a sock, a cotton ball, a block, a paperclip, and an apple
- a latex glove

Procedure:

1 Ask someone to find objects and place them in the box. Do not peek!

2 Put on the glove and put your hand through the hole. Feel the objects to try to guess what is in the box.

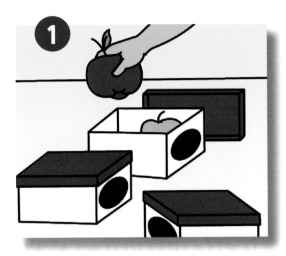

❸ Now, try again without the glove.

❹ Open the box to see what is inside.

❺ Think: Why was it harder to figure out what was in the box without your full sense of touch? What other senses would have made it easier to figure out what was in the box?

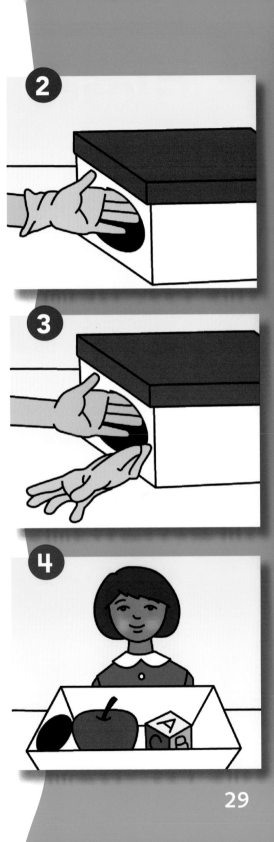

Glossary

eardrum—thin piece of skin inside the ear that is stretched tight like a drum

fingerprints—the ridges on the tip of each finger

nerves—cells that connect different parts of the body with the brain

siren—warning signal

taste buds—sensors on the tongue that let someone taste

waves—series of movements through the air

wax—sticky stuff that collects dirt inside the ears

Index

Scientists Today

Dr. Jean Bennett and Dr. Al Maguire are scientists. They are also married. They are working on ways to help blind people see.